Discover India
State by State

OFF TO MIZORAM

SONIA MEHTA

PUFFIN BOOKS

An imprint of Penguin Random House

PUFFIN BOOKS

USA | Canada | UK | Ireland | Australia | New Zealand | India | South Africa | China | Singapore

Puffin Books is part of the Penguin Random House group of companies whose addresses can be found at global.penguinrandomhouse.com

Published by Penguin Random House India Pvt. Ltd
4th Floor, Capital Tower 1, MG Road,
Gurugram 122 002, Haryana, India

First published in Puffin Books by Penguin Random House India 2018

Text, design and illustrations copyright © Quadrum Solutions Pvt. Ltd 2018
Series copyright © Penguin Random House India 2018

Picture Credits
P 6–7: Reiek, Mizoram (© Bodhisattwa [CC BY-SA 4.0 (https://creativecommons.org/licenses/by-sa/4.0)], from Wikimedia Commons);
P 7: A river in Mizoram (© Dan Markeye [CC BY 2.0 (https://creativecommons.org/licenses/by/2.0)], via Wikimedia Commons); P 9: Tam Dil Lake
(© Benjamin Rualthanzauva); P 10: Clouded leopard (© Charles Barilleaux [CC BY 2.0 (https://creativecommons.org/licenses/by/2.0)], via Wikimedia
Commons); P 12: Aizawl (© R london [CC BY-SA 3.0 (https://creativecommons.org/licenses/by/3.0)], via Wikimedia Commons), Serchhip (©
Achunga [CC BY 3.0 (https://creativecommons.org/licenses/by/3.0)], from Wikimedia Commons); P 13: Vairengte (© R london [CC BY-SA 3.0 (https://
creativecommons.org/licenses/by-sa/3.0)], via Wikimedia Commons), Vantawng Fall, Thenzawl (© Lpachuau [CC BY 3.0 (https://creativecommons.
org/licenses/by/3.0)], from Wikimedia Commons), Kolasib (© R london [CC BY-SA 3.0 (https://creativecommons.org/licenses/by-sa/3.0)], via Wikimedia
Commons); P 19: Assam–Mizoram border (© R london [CC BY-SA 3.0 (https://creativecommons.org/licenses/by-sa/3.0)], via Wikimedia Commons); P 22:
A riverside in Mizoram (© Benjamin Rualthanzauva); P 23: Girls at a Mizoram school
(© Byronkhiangte [CC BY-SA 4.0 (https://creativecommons.org/licenses/by-sa/4.0)], from Wikimedia Commons); P 31: A bamboo house
(© Benjamin Rualthanzauva), Inside a bamboo house (© Benjamin Rualthanzauva); P 32: Champhai Valley, Mizoram (© Bogman [CC BY-SA 3.0 (https://
creativecommons.org/licenses/by-sa/3.0)], from Wikimedia Commons), Kawtchhuah Ropui (© Mapuia Hnamte [CC BY-SA 3.0 (https://creativecommons.
org/licenses/by-sa/3.0)], from Wikimedia Commons); P 36: Lamsial Puk Cave (© V.L. Ramnghaka [CC BY-SA 3.0 (https://creativecommons.org/licenses/
by-sa/3.0)], from Wikimedia Commons); P 38: Lianchhiari lunglen tlang (© tourism.mizoram.gov.in), Castle of Beino (© DC Saiha [CC BY 3.0 (https://
creativecommons.org/licenses/by/3.0)], via Wikimedia Commons); P 41: Saiha, Mizoram
(© DC Saiha [CC BY 3.0 (https://creativecommons.org/licenses/by/3.0)], via Wikimedia Commons); P 44: Chhangbhan (© Lawrence Khawzawl); P 48:
Mizoram State Museum (© Irina Gelbukh [CC BY-SA 4.0 (https://creativecommons.org/licenses/by-sa/4.0)],
from Wikimedia Commons)

The views and opinions expressed in this book are the author's own and the facts are as reported by her, which have been verified to the extent
possible, and the publishers are not in any way liable for the same.

The information in this book is based on research from bona fide sites and published books and is true to the best of the author's knowledge at
the time of going to print. The author is not responsible for any further changes or developments occurring post the publication of this book.
This series is not a comprehensive representation of the states of India but is intended to give children a flavour of the lifestyles and cultures of
different states. All illustrations are artistic representations only.

ISBN 9780143440949

Design and layout by Quadrum Solutions Pvt. Ltd
Printed at Repro India Limited

www.penguin.co.in

This is a legitimate digitally printed version of the book and therefore might not
have certain extra finishing on the cover.

Hello Kids!

I'm so happy you are reading this book. India is an incredible country and there are lots of things about it that we never get to hear about.

I discovered India because my father was in the Indian army. He was posted to many places all over India—and we dutifully followed him. Can you imagine that by the time I was in the tenth standard, I had changed nine schools? Of course it was hard making new friends almost every year, but the good part was that I got to live in so many places. Right from Kerala, where I was born, to Kashmir, Jhansi, Shillong, Chandigarh, Goa . . . the list is long.

Every time I go to a new place, I feel amazed at how different each state is from the other—and yet, how similar. Did you know that we can see monuments from the Stone Age right here in India? Or that we have more than twenty official languages, and most Indians know three or four on an average? Or even that some of the world's most amazing scientific marvels were invented in India?

Oh, there are many, many, many fun and fantastic things about the states of India, which we simply must get to know.

So get your backpack ready, get set to meet some new friends and join me on a fun trip as we **DISCOVER INDIA, STATE BY STATE**.

I hope you enjoy reading this book as much as I have enjoyed writing it. I would love to hear from you. So do write to me at sonia.mehta@quadrumltd.com.

Lots of love,
Sonia Aunty

Mishki and Pushka have come to visit Earth from their home planet, Zoomba. They have never seen such an amazing place. Zoomba doesn't have trees and mountains and rivers like Earth does. But the people look exactly the same. When they come to Earth, they meet a sweet old man whom they call Daadu Dolma. Daadu Dolma shows them all the wonderful places in India and tells Mishki and Pushka all about them.

Mishki and Pushka can't believe what they see. They have seen a lot of Earth, but they have never, ever seen a place like India.

They are off to explore India state by state :)

Mishki

Mishki is a curious little girl. She is always asking loads of questions. On her home planet, she is always getting into trouble for poking her nose into things that are not her business.

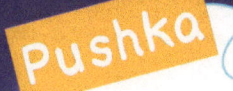

Pushka

Pushka is Mishki's brother. He loves adventure. He is always ready to try a new challenge. Whether it's climbing a mountain, or diving into a cold, cold sea, he is up for it.

Daadu Dolma

Daadu Dolma is a wise old man who has lived on Earth longer than the mountains and seas. No one knows quite how old he is, but he certainly has been around. He knows everything about everything.

Pushka wakes up extra early. He shakes Daadu Dolma and Mishki, who are both fast asleep.

'Wake up,' he says. 'Aren't we going to a state called Mizoram today? We'll be late. Hurry up!'

Mishki sits up, rubbing her eyes.

'I've already packed my things,' she says.

Daadu sits up, wide awake. 'Have you packed your binoculars?' he asks. 'You will see plenty of wildlife, because there are a lot of trees and forests where we are going.'

'I have!' exclaims Pushka. 'I've also taken my camera because I want to get some terrific pictures.'

'Well, then,' says Daadu. 'Let's be off.' They are all

OFF TO MIZORAM!!!

A SNEAK PEEK

LAND AHOY!
About the land, water, rivers, mountains and seas.
page 6

LONG, LONG AGO
The story of the state.
page 14

TALK TIME
What language do the people speak?
page 20

A PEEP INTO THEIR LIFE
The music, dance and lifestyle of the people.
page 22

BRICKS AND STONES
Of houses, buildings and bridges.
page 30

STANDING STRONG
Famous monuments in Mizoram.
page 32

WORKING HARD
What work do people do?
page 40

YUM YUM YUM
Food, food, food. What's the yummy food of Mizoram?
page 44

WHAT TO WEAR?
The clothes they wear.
page 48

AUTOGRAPH, PLEASE?
Famous people—past and present.
page 50

ONCE UPON A TIME . . .
Stories from the state.
page 54

Land ahoy!

Oh, wow! Daadu, look—so many shades of green!

Mizoram means the 'Land of the Mizos'. It used to be called the Lushai Hills District of Assam and was, for a long time, a part of Assam.

Yes, that's because you can see so many trees. Mizoram is full of forests as we'll see when we explore it.

A SMALL NEIGHBOURHOOD

Mizoram is one of the Seven Sisters, as the seven states in north-east India are known. Its sister states are Assam, Meghalaya, Manipur, Nagaland, Tripura and Arunachal Pradesh. But only three of its sisters are its neighbours—Assam, Tripura and Manipur. Its other neighbours are the countries of Myanmar (once called Burma) and Bangladesh.

UP AND DOWN

The Mizo Hills, which Mizoram is mainly made up of, are a part of the Rakhine (Arakan) mountain range. These are small ridges that run parallel to each other. They are made of rocks that are millions of years old. Narrow river valleys separate the ridges. These make the entire region full of a lot of slopes and cliffs.

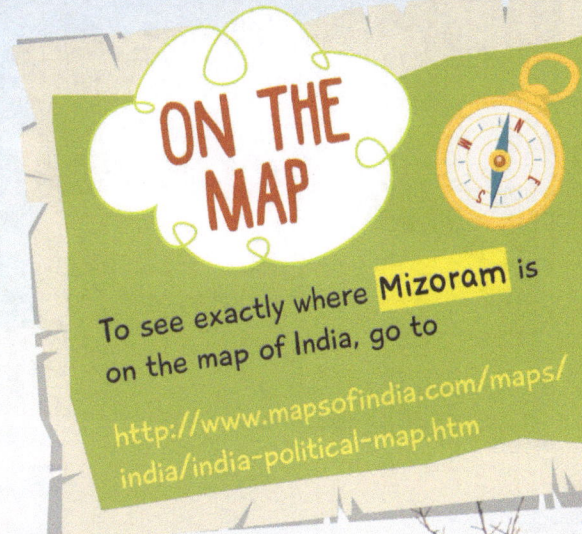

ON THE MAP

To see exactly where Mizoram is on the map of India, go to

http://www.mapsofindia.com/maps/india/india-political-map.htm

RIVER RUSH

The main river of Mizoram is the Chhimtuipui (which is also known as the Kolodyne). It has many tributaries that flow through the valleys of the Mizo hills, right into Myanmar. Some of the other rivers are the Tlawng (also called Dhaleswari), the Tuirial (also called the Sonai), as well as the Tutis and Tuivawl.

This lake is a popular tourist spot.

FORMED BY AN EARTHQUAKE

The Palak Lake, one of the largest, is said to have been created by an earthquake. Locals believe that a village once stood where the lake is today and is still submerged deep under the lake.

A SCARY LAKE

The Rih Dil (in Mizo, *rih* = heart; *dil* = lake) Lake is said to be the largest and is in the shape of a heart. It is so close to Myanmar that there is some disagreement about which country this lake actually belongs to. But its beauty is there for all to see. Legend has it that the lake is haunted. People believe that spirits pass by this lake on their way to their final resting place, *pialral* or heaven. Oooh!! Scary!

I'd hate to visit this lake at night all by myself.

THE STORY OF A MUSTARD PLANT

The Tam Dil Lake too has a story behind it. It is believed that there was an enormous mustard plant that stood tall where the lake is today. When the plant was cut down, massive jets of water spurted out and formed the lake. That's where the lake got its name from—*Tam dil* means the lake of the mustard plant.

OH, SO PLEASANT!

Mizoram has the loveliest climate. The winters are not freezing, just mild and cool enough for light woolens, and the summers are just warm, not hot. The state receives plenty of rainfall, neither too much nor too less. How lucky is that!

SUDOKU FUN

Mishki has cracked this weather Sudoku. Can you? Every row, column and small grid must have a cloud, a sun, a water drop and a snowflake. And you can't repeat any.

DAMPA
TIGER RESERVE

FOREST FANTASY

Mizoram is a truly a forest fantasy. Nearly all of it is covered with lush, green forests. Vast evergreen trees give the state plenty of forest cover, providing lots of valuable timber to people. And, of course, creating a wonderful habitat for wildlife.

ANIMALS APLENTY

The woodlands are just perfect for a wide variety of animals that roam happily in their natural habitat. Elephants, tigers, deer, bears, gibbons, monkeys and serows are just some of the wildlife this state houses. But with deforestation happening at quite an alarming rate, the government has helped build many wildlife sanctuaries in which these animals can live, free and safe and protected from poachers.

The endangered animals must be kept safe.

CROP HOP

In spite of the land being so undulating, most of the Mizos engage in farming. They grow a lot of crops, like rice and corn, many fruits, flowers and bamboo. The weather is wonderful for a vast variety of vegetables too!

FUN FACTS

State animal
Himalayan serow

State flower
Red vanda

State bird
Mrs Hume's pheasant

State tree
Indian rose chestnut

CULTIVATING CREATIVELY

It isn't easy to farm a land that is full of trees. Mizo farmers have developed two types of cultivation. One is called terrace cultivation. In this type, farmers carve out flat terraces on valley slopes and plant their crops on them. These fields are more or less permanent. The other type is called *jhum* cultivation or shifting cultivation. In this type, farmers burn trees and create a patch of land that they farm for several years. Then they move to another patch of land.

An oil palm plantation established on land traditionally used for shifting cultivation (or jhum) near Manit District.

CITY CITY BANG BANG

Mizoram's cities are not gigantic metros. They are quaint towns, and some are just a little larger than villages. Nestled in lovely scenery, these little towns have a charm of their own.

SERCHHIP

Lying in the centre of Mizoram is the city of Serchhip. It gets its name from the citrus trees that surround it, because the word *serchhip* means 'citrus on top'. It got this name because a hill in Serchhip had a citrus tree right on top of it. This city is said to have the most educated people in the state of Mizoram.

Aizawl is more than 100 years old.

AIZAWL

This city is Mizoram's capital. It's the largest city in the state and is the home of all the important offices and banks. Aizawl was an important city for the British, because it was their headquarters from where they could manage the warring tribes of the Mizo hills.

LUNGLEI

The name of this little town literally means 'a bridge of rock'. Its name comes from a rock that lies across the Nghasih river, a tributary of the Tlawng. This town is the second largest town after the capital Aizawl.

THENZAWL

This town is believed to be one of the prettiest in Mizoram. It is a major centre for the state's large handloom industry. It once was a dense forest but at some point the trees were cut down for cultivating the land. A little village was built by a man called Bengkhuaia Sailo. Over the years, it grew into a busy little town.

VAIRENGTE

This is a really small town, just a little larger than a village. When the Mizo people got together to protest for their own state, the Indian government decided to build a training centre to train soldiers to handle these protestors. A training school called the Jungle Training School was set up. Later, it was moved to Vairengte and it became an important training institute for the Indian army.

A view of the town of Kolasib

KOLASIB

This quaint little town is a wonderful getaway for tourists, because it is far away from the maddening city crowds. Surrounded by nature, it's a wonderful place to simply chill out, and people love coming here with their families for some peace and quiet.

Long, long ago

Mizoram seems like a really sweet place— nice and quiet. Was it always like this?

Oh no, not at all. Mizoram has had its share of excitement. It has had its skirmishes and battles before it became an official state of India. Come, let's jump right into its past.

AT FIRST

Mizoram is essentially a tribal state. Most of its inhabitants belong to some tribe or the other. But its origins, like those of many hilly states, are rather mysterious, because it has no clear documented history. The general belief is that the Mizos came into India as a part of a massive migration from China, thousands of years ago.

Did you know?
The word Mizoram comes from mi (people), zo (high place, such as a hill) and ram (land), and thus it means 'land of the hill people'.

A LONG JOURNEY FROM CHINA

The migrants from China had a long journey before they found a home. It is believed that they were from the Mongoloid race. When there were upheavals in China, these people found their way through thick jungles and deep valleys into Burma (now Myanmar), Mizoram's neighbour. But they found no peace there either. Their journey continued and they crossed the Tiau river and settled in the Mizo hills.

UNWELCOME VISITORS

A tribal dynasty called the Shans were ruling in the Mizo hills. They were not at all happy with their new visitors and tried to push them out, but they were unsuccessful. The Mizos lived here for over 300 years. Finally, they began to shift into the Kabaw valley, on the border of Burma.

BURMA CONNECT

The Mizos lived for a while quite happily in the Kabaw valley. There they met and interacted with the Burmese tribes. They influenced each other in their customs, food habits, clothes and culture. Some historians say that it was from the Burmese that the Mizos learnt the art of cultivation and farming.

Women from the Burmese Kayan tribe

A NEW PLACE TO SETTLE

The nomadic Mizos now found a new place to live. They built a settlement in a place called Khampat (now in Myanmar). They claimed this area as their own and went about building a town. They even built a moat around the town. They lived there for many years, until they encountered the British.

THE BRITISH ARRIVE

While the Mizos were wandering about, looking for a home, the British had been busy colonizing India. They had long had an eye on India, along with other Europeans, like the Dutch and the Portuguese. Eventually, it was the British that prevailed. They set up the East India Company, as a trading company to trade with India. But soon, it had its own troops. The British began to fight and defeat king after king in India and soon made India a British colony.

The tribes used guerilla warfare techniques to resist the British.

UNDER THE BRITISH

With India under the British, things began to become uncomfortable for the Mizos. Whenever they entered Indian territory from Burma, they were pushed back by British troops. The British, who were always seeking to expand their empire, wanted to take over Burma too. After many skirmishes, the area that the Mizos lived in became a part of the British administration. In the 1890s, finally, British formally took over the entire region, including Assam.

LUSHAI HILLS

The British were now taking action on how to manage such a large country. They divided India into regions, appointing governors to manage them. They called the entire Mizo region, with Assam, the Lushai Hills, managed by the governor of Assam.

WHAT'S ODD?

Pushka has spotted one word that's odd in each row below.
Can you spot it too?

| Assam | Uttar Pradesh | Mizoram | Nagaland | Tripura |

| Cliff | Hills | Valley | Mountain | Desert |

| Governor | Prime Minister | President | Head Chef | Chief Minister |

THE FIGHT FOR INDEPENDENCE

The people across India were not at all happy with the way the British were ruling India. They had made many rules and laws that were very unfair to Indians. There were protests and riots across India, demanding independence. Finally, things came to a head and the British gave up. In 1947, they left and India became independent.

A PART OF ASSAM

Once the British left, the Indian government had to figure out how to manage the country. They divided India into states. Many of these states were formed, on the basis of language. Assam became a state and Mizoram was a part of it. For many years, it remained so.

THEIR OWN MIZO STATE

The Mizos were not too happy with this arrangement. They were proud of their culture and identity. They felt that their culture was distinct and unique. They wanted their own state. They formed an organization called the Mizo National Front and began demanding that Mizoram become a state in its own right.

Assam

Mizoram

A STATE AT LAST

Finally, after years of rebellion, in 1986 the government signed the Mizoram Peace Accord. And after so much wandering and wondering, Mizoram became a state on 20 February 1987. Whew!

ELCOME TO IZORAM
State Bank of India
The banker to every Indian

The Mizos are very proud of their land and their culture.

Talk time

What an interesting history! I'd like to meet some Mizo people now, and speak to them.

A TOUCH OF CHINA

The main language (apart from English) spoken by the tribes of Mizoram is Mizo Tawng, or simply Mizo. This language is a Sino-Tibetan language (which means it has Chinese and Tibetan roots). Some also call this language Lushai. But thanks to the British and the many missionaries who came to Mizoram to spread the message of Jesus Christ, English is very widely spoken here. It's also the official language. But many people from Mizoram are arguing for Mizo to become the official state language.

Well, you can. It'll be easy because most of them know English. But if you'd like to speak in their language, you will have to learn Mizo Tawng.

- Hello = Chibai
- Good morning = Zing chibai
- Have a nice day = Ni hman nuam le
- Good evening = Tlailam chibai
- Good night = Mangṭha
- Sleep tight = Tui deuhin i mu dawnnia
- Thank you = Ka läwm e
- How are you? = I dam em?
- Welcome = Kan/Ka läwm a che
- Congratulations = Ka lawm pui a che
- Happy birthday = Piancham chibai

WORD MATCH

Can you remember the new Mizo words you've learnt? Match the English phrases to their Mizo meanings.

Good night	Ka läwm pui a che
Thank you	I dam em?
Congratulations	Chibai
Happy birthday	Ka läwm e
Hello	Mangṭha
How are you?	Piancham chibai

A peep into their life

I'd love to meet the people now and get to know all about their customs.

Well, then, what are we waiting for? You're going to love the colourful and cheerful Mizos.

A MIXED BAG

The Mizos have really had an eventful past. They came from China, lived in Burma for several hundred years, then became a part of Assam before finally having their own state. So you can just imagine how many different cultures and traditions they would have imbibed over the years. Thanks to the missionaries who came to north-east India, many converted to Christianity.

Traditionally, the Mizos followed an animistic religion, which means they believed that everything— trees, objects, plants— have a soul.

MANY TRIBES— BUT ONE IDENTITY

There are many sub-tribes living in Mizoram. Luseis, Lais, Maras, Kukis are some. They all have their own customs and traditions. Together, they are known as the Mizos. Thanks to the missionaries, the Mizos are one of the most educated communities in India.

CELEBRATING HARVEST

Harvest is one of the biggest events in Mizoram, because most of the people are farmers. There are several harvest festivals the people celebrate. *Mim kut* and *Pawi kut* are two such festivals. During Mim kut, people also honour their ancestors who are no longer alive. Both festivals involve a whole lot of music, song and dance. And, of course, feasts.

PREPARING FOR JHUM

Chapchar kut is an ancient festival of Spring, to celebrate the completion of the preparation of land for jhum. It was revived in 1973 to uphold Mizo tradition. Traditionally it involved home-brewed alcohol and meat delicacies. Nowadays, it involves the *Cheraw* and *Chai* dances, along with feasting, and is much anticipated all over the state.

The dances in Mizoram are full of life. People dress up in traditional costumes and dance their cares away.

CHERAW

This ancient dance is similar to some tribal dances in other Asian countries. This is the most popular dance in Mizoram. It's also called the Bamboo Dance. Two rows of men, facing each other, tap together long bamboo sticks that are placed in a criss-cross pattern, creating small squares of space in between that will shut the moment the sticks are moved. Women in bright costumes hop skilfully in and out between the bamboo sticks in tune with the rhythm. This dance needs a lot of skill and is simply amazing to watch.

SARLAMKAI

This is a dramatic victory dance. In the olden days, the victorious tribe would perform this dance to ensure that the enemy remained enslaved even after their death. This dance is a part of a long festival that goes on for around five days. There is no song—only the dramatic beating of gongs and drums. Boys and girls in colourful attire dance in circles while the lead dancer is dressed as a warrior.

CHAILAM

This dance is performed during Chapchar kut with the men and women dancing in a circle to music played with drums and a mithun's horn. There are four—five versions of this dance. Legend has it that once a tribal king was very despondent after an unsuccessful hunt, so his people performed this dance to cheer him up.

A mithun's horn

CHAWNGLAIZAWN

This dance is performed on one of two occasions. When a husband loses his wife, he performs this dance till he is exhausted, after which his friends and relatives dance in his stead. It is an expression of grief. The other occasion is when hunters return from a hunt with their trophy. Isn't it strange that the same dance has two opposite meanings?

SHADOW PLAY

Look at these dancers doing the Cheraw dance. Can you find their exact shadow?

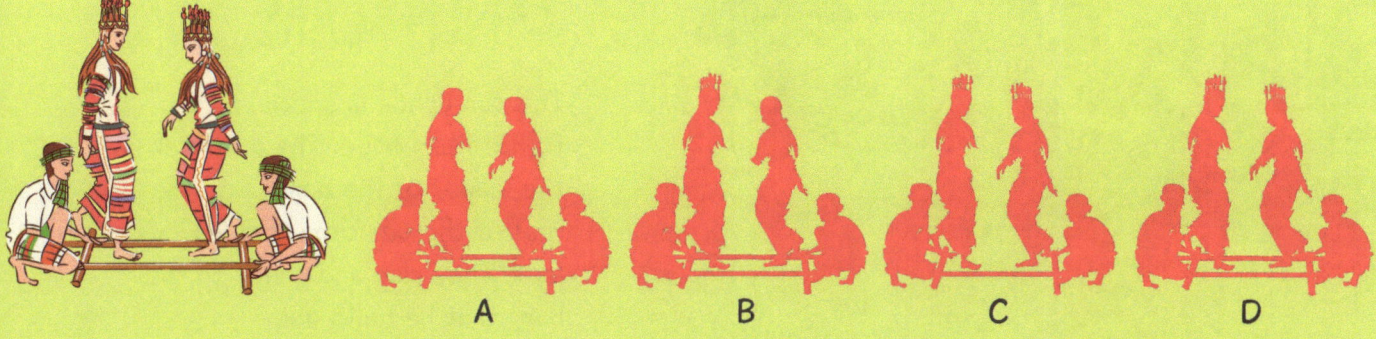

A   B   C   D

TLANGLAM

Both men and women perform this hugely popular dance. There are many versions of this dance, but when you say Mizo, this is the dance that comes to mind. In fact, there are cultural troupes that perform this dance all over the country too!

CHHEIHLAM

Chheihlam is different from Chailam though they sound similar. This is a dance of joy, performed to a song called *Chheih Hla*. The dancers squat on the ground in a circle and to the vigorous beat of bamboo sticks or drums, they sing and perform this dance. Many of the songs are made up on the spot. This dance is generally performed in the evening.

The drummer decides how long the dance will last. Sounds fun!

ZANGTALAM

This fun dance is special to the Paihte Mizo tribe. The drummer is the leader of the dance and the rest of the performers follow his lead. They clap and dance to the beat that he belts out.

PAR LAM DANCE

Here's a pretty dance! The women put on pretty dresses, tuck flowers in their hair and dance to the music of the guitars being played by the men. Isn't that lovely?

Awesome fun!

THE
DANCE GRID

There are six Mizo dances hidden in this grid. Can you find them all?

A	W	E	R	T	Y	U	I	I	O	P	A	S
C	H	A	W	N	G	L	A	I	Z	A	W	N
A	S	A	R	L	A	M	K	A	I	V	T	N
A	D	D	C	H	E	R	A	W	Q	Z	X	C
C	H	H	E	I	H	L	A	M	S	D	F	H
W	E	T	L	A	N	G	L	A	M	A	S	D
P	A	R	L	A	M	Z	X	C	V	B	Y	O

MUSIC TIME

The music of Mizoram is just as enchanting as its dances. Did you know that there are different kinds of music and chants—each with a different purpose?

TIME TO CELEBRATE

The songs people sing when they are celebrating and making merry are called the *Puipun Hla* songs. These songs are very popular and are sung and danced to on any joyous occasion.

A VICTORY CHANT

When warriors return victorious from battle, *Bawh Hla* is the cry or chant they raise in order to announce their superiority over their enemy. Usually, the most successful warrior, who has vanquished the most people from the enemy ranks, raises this cry.

WHEN INSTRUMENTS SING

Dar Hla are songs made by musical instruments only. Dar hla means 'the song of the gong'. People believe that instruments are actually singing.

NAMED AFTER TRIBES

Some songs are named after tribes; for example, *Sailo Zai* and *Saivate Zai*.

NAMED AFTER VILLAGES

There are also songs named after villages. They were probably developed in a particular village and became popular. *Lumtui Zai* and *Dar Lung Zai* are two examples.

CHANT OF THE HUNTER

Hlado is a hunting chant. After a successful hunt, hunters carry their prey back triumphantly chanting the Hlado all the way home into the village.

Lengzem zai are love songs! These are songs that tell tales of love and longing.

FEELING RELIGIOUS

Thiam Hla and *Dawi Hla* are two kinds of chants that only priests recite—when they perform a religious ceremony or a ritual.

RHYME TIME

Mishki has written a lovely poem about Mizoram. Can you help her complete it?

There's music in the Mizo hills
When I hear it, my heart ______
With the joy I get to hear them sing
Music is a lovely ______
It makes you happy, when you're sad
Raises your spirits when you're feeling
______
I love the music of the Mizo hills
Even more than roller-coaster ______

Did you know?
There are also songs named after composers. And there are some that are named after a village chief, or the village beauty. How sweet!

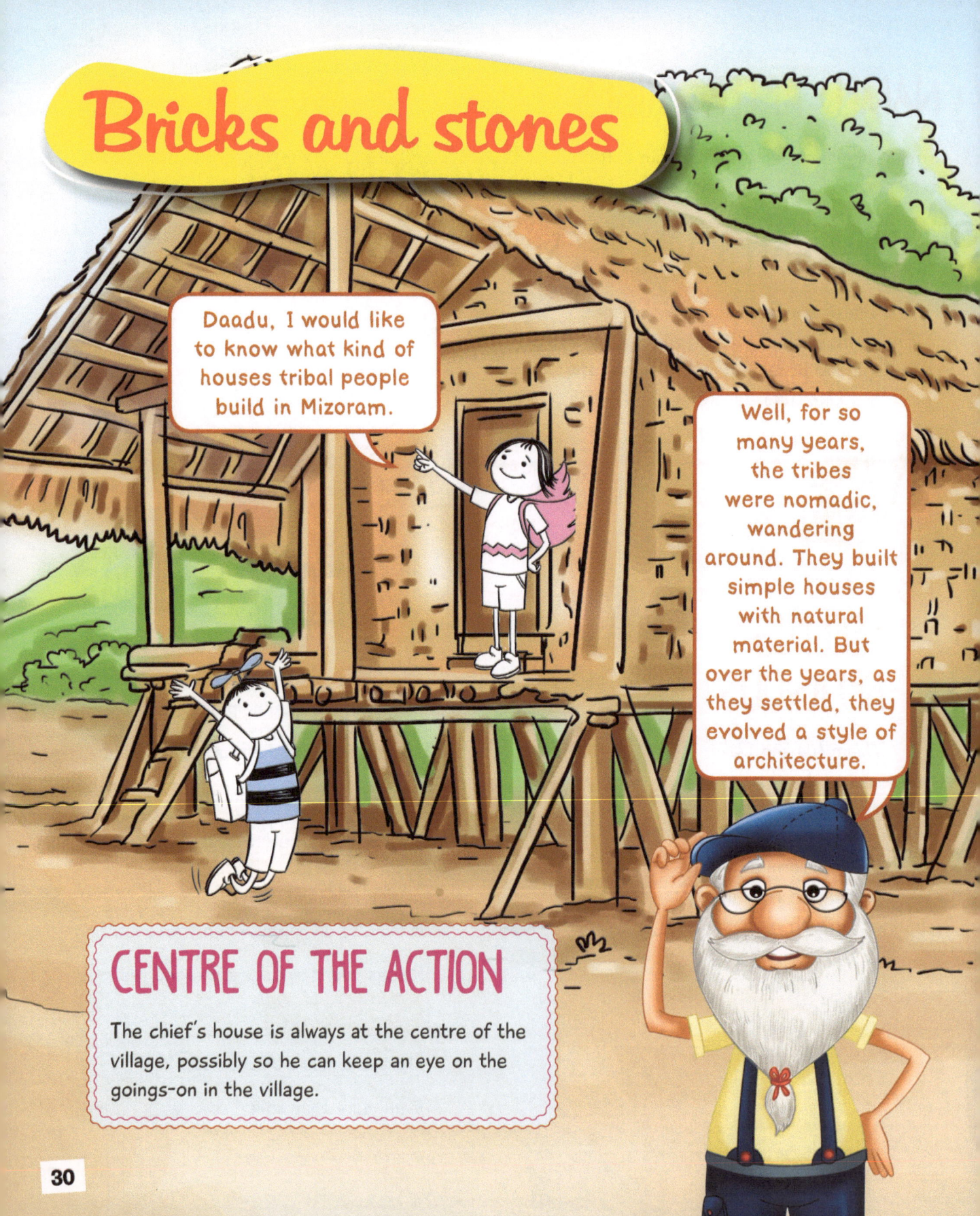

Bricks and stones

Daadu, I would like to know what kind of houses tribal people build in Mizoram.

Well, for so many years, the tribes were nomadic, wandering around. They built simple houses with natural material. But over the years, as they settled, they evolved a style of architecture.

CENTRE OF THE ACTION

The chief's house is always at the centre of the village, possibly so he can keep an eye on the goings-on in the village.

SPECIAL QUARTERS FOR BACHELORS

Many tribes in north-eastern India have this system of a special house for young, unmarried men. In Mizoram, these homes are called *zawlbuk*. The young men living here also get their education in hunting and the ways of the tribe from the elders of the tribe.

HOUSE OF BAMBOO

The houses are often built on stilts. Some houses are built on slopes so they have stilts only on one side. There's usually a front or a back veranda. Invariably, the material people use is the abundant bamboo, along with wood.

OH SO HIGH!

As much as possible, people like to build their homes on a hilltop. This was probably because it gave them a clear view of approaching enemies. Now it's just a premium spot.

ROOMS WITH SCREENS

Inside the houses, people create rooms simply by putting cane or bamboo matted screens. The shelves, beds and other furniture are made of cane and bamboo.

Standing strong

I think this state is lovely. I can't wait to see its monuments!

The monuments here are a little different from what you see in many other parts of India. They are not grand pieces of architecture, but much simpler, though just as meaningful. And many of them are natural monuments.

KAWTCHHUAH ROPUI

This means the Great Entranceway. This is a heritage site, at a place called Khawbung. It's made of more than 170 carved menhir stones. Each stone is a memorial to a loved one, who may have been a great warrior or have done something great in his lifetime.

It's set in the midst of lovely woodland and makes for a lovely visit.

SIBUTA LUNG

This is a memorial stone in a village near Aizawl. Legend goes that a young orphan called Sibuta was adopted by the chief of the village. But Sibuta was greedy for power and killed his father and became chief. He fell in love with a maiden, who would not have him. Furious, he buried the girl in a pit and decided to build a memorial for himself on the pit. He got a gigantic stone pulled from the depths of the river and built this memorial to himself. Quite a story!!!

MANGKHAIA LUNG

This massive structure is also a memorial stone. It has detailed engravings of human figures as well as animals. People believe that these figures are the guardians of people who have died. Tribal culture is certainly full of beliefs and superstitions.

AN ENTIRE VILLAGE

Quite close to Aizawl, you can see a typical Mizo village of the olden days. The village has been specially created to show people how the tribes lived so many years ago. You can see the house of the chief, the blacksmith's hut, the bachelors' dormitory and all the things that a village had.

Did you know?
There's also a memorial stone that was created in honour of the martyrs who fought against the British.

LUNGPHUN LIAN

In the district of Champhai is a village named Lungphun lian. It is named after an enormous monolith that is said to be probably the largest in all of Mizoram. No one knows what this stands for, but its sheer size has made it something quite unique.

LUNGDING

This means 'upright stone'. This is a fascinating natural rock that is more than 60 feet tall. It's covered with shrubs. What's special about it is that in the ancient days the Mizos believed that spirits lived in these rocks. They used to pray to this rock. Many years later, even after most converted to Christianity, this rock is still considered sacred.

UI LUNG

This is an enormous monolith with intricate carvings all over it of animal heads, gongs and drums and human figures carrying weapons like knives and spears. It depicts the life people lived in those days.

Oh wow! That's enormous!

LUNG MILEM

Here's a mystery! Though there is no record of any Buddhist influence in Mizoram, this rock has the carving of three figures meditating in a Buddhist pose. Lung Milem literally means figures of stone.

JUMBLED UP

Pushka is trying to unjumble the words he's just heard. Can you help him?

1. The Ui Lung monolith has weapons like knives and **SRSEAP** carved on it.

2. The Lung Milem monolith seems to have a **DUDBISHT** influence.

3. The Mizos believed that **IISRPTS** lived in the Lungding rocks.

4. The Mangkhaia Lung monolith has carvings of humans and **LAMISNA** all over it.

5. The Sibuta Lung monolith has a legend in which Sibuta was adopted by the tribal **FIHCE**.

SHOUTING CAVE

Puk Zing is a 'cave of a shouting stone'. That is what the name means, and of course there's a story behind it. This roomy cave has three chambers. Legend says that villagers used to hear evil spirits shouting inside the cave.

LAMSIAL PUK CAVE

This incredible cave has its own mystery. It's said that deep in the cave is a wooden box that is full of tightly packed, and nicely preserved . . . HUMAN BONES!!! Whoa! That's weird isn't it? It's a mystery because no one knows for sure who the bones belong to and why they are there. But it's eerie, all right!

PEOPLE SAY that some religious rites must have been performed here years and years ago!

MURA PUK

This is a group of six caves that are said to have been made by man. Tribals say that in the olden days, there was a giant eagle that would attack unsuspecting people. The caves were created to hide from this nasty eagle.

KUNGAWRHI PUK

This is a deep and very wide hole on the mountainside. People say that this was the entrance to a hidden underground village in which spirits lived. People visit it even today.

HIDDEN WORDS

Like the caves are hidden on the mountainsides, Pushka has found ten words hidden in the name. How many can you find?

KUNGAWRHI PUK

<u>HANG</u> _____ _____ _____

_____ _____ _____

_____ _____

FIARA TUI

Let's start with the story. Many many years ago there was a terrible drought and people travelled far to get water. Fiara, the son of a poor widow, happened to look below a flat stone. To his amazement, he found a deep and crystal clear pool of water. The widow and her son kept this source a secret for many years. Finally, it was discovered by other villagers. They say the water from this hidden pool is sweeter than any water anywhere.

LIANCHHIARI LUNGLEN TLANG

This legendary cliff sticks out at an angle from a mountainside. Legend goes that a maiden called Lianchhiari would wait for her lover, Chawngfiang, and sit mournfully on this rock cliff. The cliff inspires local poets to write delightful love songs.

CASTLE OF BEINO

This is an amazing rock formation that looks like a castle. From the middle of the serene river Chhimtuipui rises this rock structure, carved by nature. The local people believe that the River Queen of Spirits lives in this castle.

LOST IN A MAZE

Mishki and Pushka are lost in Kawtchhuah Ropui. Can you help them find their way to Daadu Dolma?

Working hard

I know what you are both thinking. That you would like to live here forever.

How did you guess? I think this is a great place to settle down, isn't it?

But then we would need to know how to earn some money. I'm sure Daadu is going to tell us all about what people do here.

FARMER, FARMER, WHAT DO YOU GROW?

As we've seen, farming is the most important activity here and most of the tribes earn their livelihood through farming. Apart from rice and maize, farmers grow a special kind of ginger called fibreless ginger. They also grow mustard, sugarcane, potatoes and grapes. Between growing these crops, and clearing land for cultivation, farmers are kept very busy all right!

SMALL BUSINESSES

There are many small businesses that people run, called small-scale industries. These are run at the village level. Producing silk, manufacturing furniture, refining oil, processing ginger—all these are part of this.

TOURIST TRENDS

The natural beauty of Mizoram attracts lots of tourists who come here to enjoy the state's natural beauty. There are many people who work in hotels, restaurants and travel agencies to make sure that tourists are looked after.

TWIN GINGERS

Look at the ginger that Mizoram is so famous for. Can you find two pieces of ginger that are exactly alike?

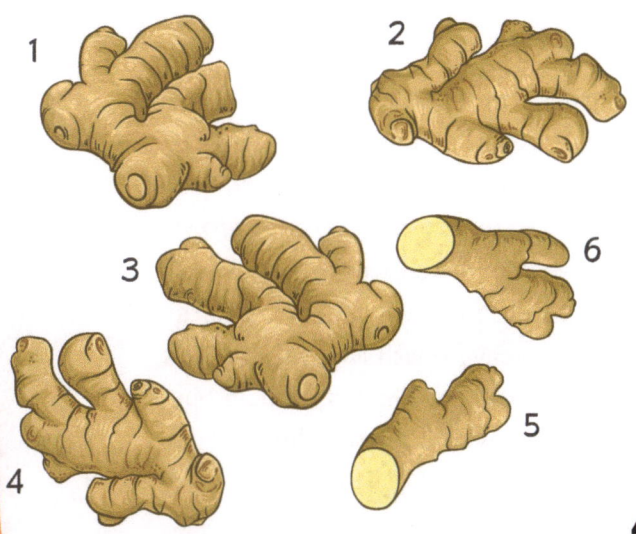

1
2
3
6
4
5

HANDY HANDICRAFT

Mizoram's handicrafts are famous all over the world and the people are a really talented lot. Let's see what kind of things they make.

Living in forests and making do with the natural material available to them has made people really creative.

BASKET GALORE

Basketry is really popular in Mizoram. For generations, the tribal people have been using the soft cane and bamboo that grows there to make lovely baskets. There are many types of baskets they weave—with lids, without lids and in various shapes. People buy these baskets all over India.

WEAVING WONDERS

The tribal people of Mizoram are expert weavers—especially the women. They weave lovely shawls, jackets, mats, rugs and lots of other things. The Mizo fabric is very bright and very popular in the country.

SPOT THE
DIFFERENCES

Look at the lovely weave of this basket. Can you find ten places where the weave has gone wrong?

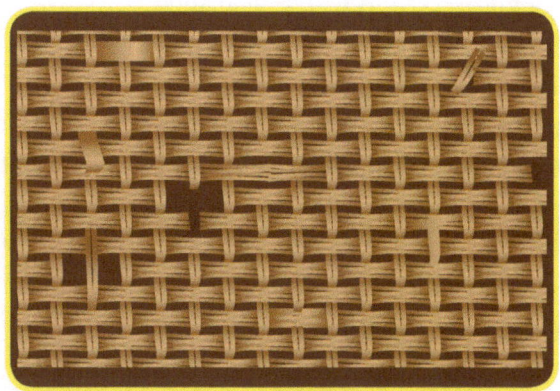

Yum yum yum

Yay! Is it time for food? I can smell some lovely fragrant aromas. What's cooking?

You are going to love the Mizo cuisine. Some of it has become really popular in other states. And some of it is common to its six sisters too! Are you ready for the foodie journey?

CHHANGBAN LEH KURTAI

It's easier to cook this dish than pronounce it. It's made with just rice flour and jaggery, and is steamed all wrapped up in leaves. Wow! That's healthy.

BAI

This yummy soup-like dish is available in almost every Mizo home. It's made with meat, vegetables and bamboo shoots. It has the unique flavour of Mizo spices. It makes a great start to a meal—and even a great meal all by itself.

KOAT PITHA

This crunchy dish is made of rice flour and guess what—bananas! Some people also add fish to it. Strange combination isn't it? But the local people love it. They enjoy it with Zu, special Mizo tea.

BAMBOO SHOOT FRY

Vegetarians can rejoice. Bamboo shoot fry is one of the few entirely vegetarian dishes. Bamboo shoots are fried and tossed in spices, sometimes along with mushrooms. It's a super tasty dish.

PANCH PHORAN TARKA

This dish can be veggie too, although most people cook it with chicken. The vegetarian version sounds nice and healthy as it has pumpkin, brinjal and potato. It's spicy, so you need to eat it carefully.

MISA MAAS POORA

If you love shrimp, you're in for treat. This dish is a glorious blend of shrimp and vegetables. People love to have it with rice.

HMARCHA RAWT

Here's a spicy chutney that will leave your eyes watering. It's got plenty of chillies—red or green—that are ground together. Then, topped with ginger and raw onion, it adds that special zing to any meal.

CHHUM HAN

Here's another veggie delight—that is super healthy too. A whole lot of vegetables like cabbage, carrots and tomatoes are steamed with ginger and salt. It's a delicious stew that can be eaten along with rice.

ZU

There's a unique kind of tea that the Mizos love to have. It's called *zu*. It has a different taste from the tea we commonly have, but the Mizos swear by it. Must try it!

FOOD GRID

Mishki and Pushka are making a super spread. They need a lot of vegetables and fruit. Can you find ten vegetables and ten fruits hidden in this grid? You can look sideways and from up to down too!

Z	K	K	J	H	G	F	D	S	A	B	D	S	B	A
X	L	A	D	Y	F	I	N	G	E	R	Q	W	A	T
C	V	P	B	Z	X	B	C	V	N	O	R	E	N	G
C	Z	P	E	A	R	G	F	D	S	C	S	A	A	H
U	M	L	M	A	N	G	O	N	C	O	P	K	N	P
C	N	E	B	V	X	C	V	B	M	C	I	L	A	A
U	Q	W	A	T	E	R	M	E	L	O	N	J	H	P
M	A	S	D	B	R	I	N	J	A	L	A	F	G	A
B	L	K	J	H	G	F	K	I	W	I	C	G	D	Y
E	Z	G	R	A	P	E	S	Z	A	S	H	U	Z	A
R	Q	S	C	D	F	G	H	J	K	L	B	A	X	A
A	O	R	A	N	G	E	E	W	Q	M	N	V	C	V
S	D	F	B	G	H	J	K	R	T	O	M	A	T	O
S	D	F	B	G	H	Z	X	C	V	B	K	J	H	H
P	O	T	A	T	O	H	C	A	R	R	O	T	W	Q
A	S	D	G	F	G	N	M	A	S	D	H	G	F	D
F	G	H	E	C	A	U	L	I	F	L	O	W	E	R

What to wear?

Daadu, I'd love to try on some of those interesting tribal costumes.

Well then what are you waiting for? The clothes people wear in Mizoram are very colourful. They're creative too.

WOVEN SPLENDOUR

Originally, the garment both men and women wore was called a *puan*. This was an intricately woven piece, woven by women with great attention to detail. There would be patterns and motifs that held special meaning for the women and their families.

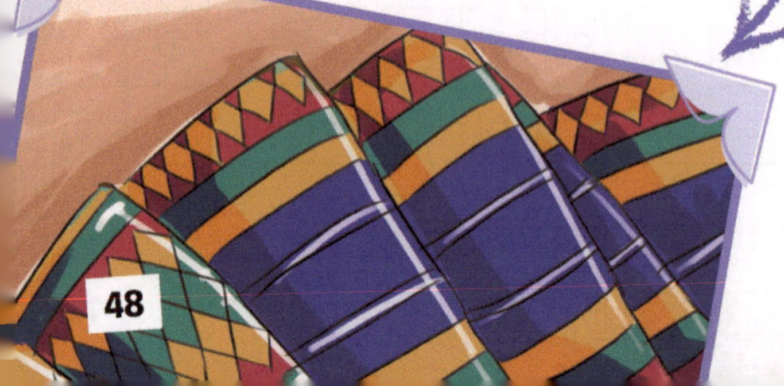

ZAKUOLAISEN

This is a dress worn by unmarried girls. It's a riot of dramatic coloured stripes.

48

NGOTEKHERH

This is a long cloth draped around the body, like a sarong. Both men and women wear this, but drape it differently.

PUANCHEI

This is the main garment Mizo women wear. It's a colourful garment and is something like a sarong.

The girls in Mizoram are creative. They have made their traditional dress into a fashion statement.

KAWRCHEI

The *paunchei* is worn with a colourful blouse called a *kawrchei*.

TRIBAL MEN

Mizo men have a simple style of dressing. The most common is a long cloth, draped around the waist. During winter, this is teamed with a white coat. Some men wear the cloth only up to the knees. And sometimes, they add a turban or a bandana to the whole outfit.

Autograph, please?

Are there many celebrities from this state, Daadu?

Mizoram has some very accomplished people. They may not be as famous as some of the other celebrities in India, but their achievements are just as amazing.

LALDENGA

He started the Mizo National Front, which fought so hard for Mizoram to become a state. He went on to become the first chief minister of Mizoram. He was a soldier in the Indian army before he became a rebel to the cause of Mizoram's statehood.

LALSANGZUALI SAILO

This talented lady was not only a poet and writer, she was also a gospel singer and music composer. She was highly educated and highly respected in the Mizo community.

Gospel singers are talented performers who sing in churches.

JEJE LALPEKHLUA

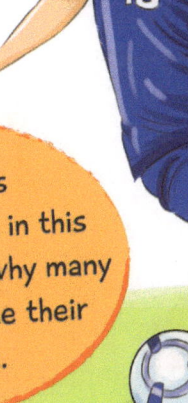

Here's a footballer who has played for India. He is known to have scored many goals that have helped India win in international football matches. He is one of the highest goal scorers in the Indian Super League.

Football is a popular sport in this region. Which is why many youngsters make their mark in it.

LALRINDIKA RALTE

He is a popular footballer who is known affectionately as Dika. He plays in the Indian Super League for the Northeast United team.

I'd love to see them play!

People
Maze

Can you help Pushka follow the people box maze by only following the people from Mizoram?

SPOT THE CELEBRITIES

Pushka and Mishki are celebrity spotting. They know some celebrities, but aren't sure of some. How many can you name?

I could do with some help.

Once upon a time . . .

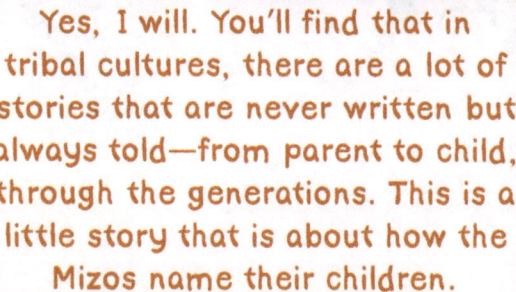

Wow! That was a super trip. But before we go off to the next state, will you be telling us a story from Mizoram? Like you always do?

WHAT'S IN A NAME?

Yes, I will. You'll find that in tribal cultures, there are a lot of stories that are never written but always told—from parent to child, through the generations. This is a little story that is about how the Mizos name their children.

Many, many years ago, the Mizo people believed that a long name brought good fortune. So the longer the name, the greater the fortune that the family got.

Whenever a child was born, the elders would get together and think of the longest, loveliest name they could come up with. This was especially important for the first born. So the eldest child always had the longest name ever.

And so it was in the little family that our story is about.

The couple in our story was blessed with two boys. As was the custom, the older boy had a long name. His name was Tala Bini Bendo Toko Miki Sembu Chima Chimena Kit Kit Kuki Mizi Pizi Hala. Whew! That's a long name, all right. Tala Bini Bendo Toko Miki Sembu Chima Chimena Kit Kit Kuki Mizi Pizi Hala's parents and grandparents were very pleased with the name. So when the second son was born, they simply named him Semu.

The two brothers enjoyed playing about in the forest, like all young boys of the tribe did. They loved doing naughty things like climb up trees and jump off them.

One day, as they were playing, Semu climbed up a tall tree next to a well. 'I can jump off this tree and land on my feet,' he boasted.

'You can't,' his brother Tala Bini Bendo Toko Miki Sembu Chima Chimena Kit Kit Kuki Mizi Pizi Hala retorted.

'I can too,' replied Semu. He climbed right to the top of the tree and took a flying leap.

And unfortunately for him, SPLASH he fell into the deep well.

Tala Bini Bendo Toko Miki Sembu Chima Chimena Kit Kit Kuki Mizi Pizi Hala was horrified. He ran to the house.

'Mother,' he yelled. 'Semu has fallen into the well.'

Their mother came rushing out. She called some of the youth who were working in a nearby bamboo grove.

'Oh, please, come and help pull Semu out of the well,' she cried. A couple of young men came and, in no time, Semu was pulled out of the well, safe and sound.

A few days went by. The boys had been warned to stay away from the well. But boys will be boys! And soon, they were both challenging each other to see who would jump further.

This time it was Tala Bini Bendo Toko Miki Sembu Chima Chimena Kit Kit Kuzi Mizi Pizi Hala who was being challenged.

'I bet you can't jump as far or as high as I can,' challenged Semu.

'Of course, I can,' replied Tala Bini Bendo Toko Miki Sembu Chima Chimena Kit Kit Kuzi Mizi Pizi Hala. 'Just watch me.'

He climbed a tree and leapt with all his might. And just as his brother had, he too fell SPLASH into the deep well. Semu sprung into action.

'Mother, mother,' he yelled. 'Tala Bini Bendo Toko Miki Sembu Chima Chimena Kit Kit Kuzi Mizi Pizi Hala has fallen into the well.'

His mother was washing clothes and did not hear.

'What did you say?' she called out.

'I said, Tala Bini Bendo Toko Miki Sembu Chima Chimena Kit Kit Kuzi Mizi Pizi Hala has fallen into the well,' Semu shouted back.

This time she heard. She dropped her washing and rushed to call for help.

'Help! Help!' she hollered. 'Tala Bini Bendo Toko Miki Sembu Chima Chimena Kit Kit Kuzi Mizi Pizi Hala has fallen into the well!'

By the time she could say her son's entire name, it was too late. When the villagers rescued the boy from the well, Tala Bini Bendo Toko Miki Sembu Chima Chimena Kit Kit Kuzi Mizi Pizi Hala was unconscious. The village doctor had to be called and it took weeks and weeks for him to recover.

And it was all because his name was so long.

Ever since, it is said, the Mizos make sure the names of their children are nice and short.

TRAVEL DIARY

Have you enjoyed this trip to Mizoram with your friends Mishki and Pushka—and, of course, with Daadu Dolma?

Now you can make your own Mizoram diary. And if you ever visit Mizoram, make sure you take pictures and put them in the photo box.

The first place I would visit in Mizoram:

_____

If I could perform one of the folk dances, I would dance:

_____

The one dish I am definitely going to eat:

_____

The monument I think is the most interesting:

_____

The one famous person from Mizoram I would love to meet:

_____

The tribe from Mizoram I would like to dress up as:

_____

The festival from Mizoram that I think is the most fun:

_____

The five words that I think describe Mizoram the best are:

_____

_____

_____

_____

_____

My Mizoram memories:

ANSWERS

page 9 SUDOKU FUN

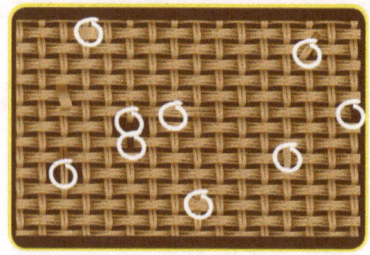

page 17 WHAT'S ODD?

UTTAR PRADESH, DESERT, HEAD CHEF

Page 21 WORD MATCH

Good night—Mangţha; Thank you—Ka läwm e; Congratulations—Ka lawm pui a che; Happy birthday—Piancham chibai; Hello—Chibai; How are you?—I dam em?

Page 25 SHADOW PLAY

D

page 27 THE DANCE GRID

A	W	E	R	T	Y	U	I	I	O	P	A	S
C	H	A	W	N	G	L	A	I	Z	A	W	N
A	S	A	R	L	A	M	K	A	I	V	T	N
A	D	D	C	H	E	R	A	W	Q	Z	X	C
C	H	H	E	I	H	L	A	M	S	D	F	H
W	E	T	L	A	N	G	L	A	M	A	S	D
P	A	R	L	A	M	Z	X	C	V	B	Y	O

Page 29 RHYME TIME

fills, thing, bad, thrills

Page 35 JUMBLED UP

SPEARS, BUDDHIST, SPIRITS, ANIMALS, CHIEF

Page 37 HIDDEN WORDS

Here are some of the words that you can form: ring, hang, wag, rag, king, wing, wink, pink, raw, paw, park

Page 39 LOST IN A MAZE

Page 41 TWIN GINGERS

2 and 4 are same

Page 43 SPOT THE DIFFERENCES

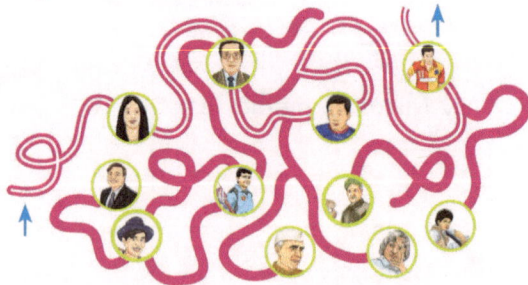

Page 47 FOOD GRID

Z	K	K	J	H	G	F	D	S	A	B	D	S	B	A
X	L	A	D	Y	F	I	N	G	E	R	Q	W	A	T
C	V	P	B	Z	X	B	C	V	N	O	R	E	N	G
C	Z	P	E	A	R	G	F	D	S	C	S	A	A	H
U	M	L	M	A	N	G	O	N	C	O	P	K	N	P
C	N	E	B	V	X	C	V	B	M	C	I	L	A	A
U	Q	W	A	T	E	R	M	E	L	O	N	J	H	P
M	A	S	D	B	R	I	N	J	A	L	A	F	G	A
B	L	K	J	H	G	F	K	I	W	I	C	G	D	Y
E	Z	G	R	A	P	E	S	Z	A	S	H	U	Z	A
R	Q	S	C	D	F	G	H	J	K	L	B	A	X	A
A	O	R	A	N	G	E	E	W	Q	M	N	V	C	V
S	D	F	B	G	H	J	K	R	T	O	M	A	T	O
S	D	F	B	G	H	Z	X	C	V	B	K	J	H	H
P	O	T	A	T	O	H	C	A	R	R	O	T	W	Q
A	S	D	G	F	G	N	M	A	S	D	H	G	F	D
F	G	H	E	C	A	U	L	I	F	L	O	W	E	R

Page 51 PEOPLE MAZE

page 52—53 SPOT THE CELEBRITIES

Dalai Lama, Sachin Tendulkar, Lakshmi Mittal, Rajnikanth, Laldenga, Kalpana Chawla, Pawan Chamling, Kapil Dev, Rabindranath Tagore, Prabhas, Raj Kapoor, Lalsangzuali Sailo, Jawaharlal Nehru, Rahul Dravid, Dr APJ Abdul Kalam.